Honey, Does This Make My Butt Look Big?

A Couple's Guide to Food and Body Talk

LYDIA HANICH, MA, LMFT

gürze books

Honey, Does This Make My Butt Look Big?
A Couples Guide to Food and Body Talk
© 2005 by Lydia Hanich, MS, LMFT

Gürze Books
P.O. Box 2238
Carlsbad, CA 92018
800-756-7533
www.gurze.com

Cover design by Johnson Design
Cover photo © Getty Images

Illustrations: NON SEQUITUR © 1998, 1999, 2001 & 2002 Wiley Miller,
Dist. By UNIVERSAL PRESS SYNDICATE
Reprinted with permission. All rights reserved.

Library of Congress Cataloging-in-Publication Data
Hanich, Lydia, 1957-
  Honey, does this make my butt look big? : a couples guide to food and body talk
/ by Lydia Hanich.
      p. cm.
   ISBN-13: 978-0-936077-24-6
   ISBN-10: 0-936077-24-7
   1. Eating disorders in women--Psychological aspects. 2. Overweight women--Family relationships. 3. Body image in women. 4. Husbands--Attitudes. 5. Husbands--Psychology. 6. Man-woman relationships. I. Title.
   RC552.E18H368 2005
   362.196'8526--dc22
2005028770

Printed on recycled paper

NOTE
The author and publisher of this book intend for this publication to provide accurate information. It is sold with the understanding that it is meant to complement, not substitute for, professional medical and/or psychological services.

2 4 6 8 0 9 7 5 3 1

To my sweet,
beloved husband,
Robert G. Field

CONTENTS

"Honey, Does This Make My Butt Look Big?"

You hear these words and freeze in your tracks. You get a sinking feeling in your stomach. What to do? How to answer? Do you lie? Tell the truth? Pretend you didn't hear? Try to distract her? Your instincts tell you to run. It's fight or flight, and you'd much rather flee because you've stayed for the fight before, and you know you can't win. With a seemingly simple question, your honey has catapulted you into a complete quandary and rendered you utterly defenseless. You're cornered, trapped. You'd rather gnaw off a foot than answer that question. Talk about a loaded question! You HATE that question! There's only one place it has ever led you: trouble. And there's been no way out of the trap...until now.

First, let me assure you that you are not alone in this quandary. As a psychotherapist specializing in the treatment of eating disorders and body image issues (predominantly among women), I have repeatedly encountered the frustration, confusion, and helplessness felt by many husbands and boyfriends of my clients. While completely

sincere in their desire to support their honey's recovery, too often they unwittingly say or do something that exacerbates the problem rather than contributing to the solution. Their best intentions can banish them to a night on the couch. They become secondary victims of the eating and body image problems that plague American women today. The vast majority of them are baffled and confounded by the whole thing, particularly their role in it. Relationships are often strained, if not damaged, by this unhealthy dynamic. If you are one of these men, the first six chapters of this book are for you and your relationship.

In our society, males and females have been acculturated from an early age to believe that their essential value derives from very different sources. While young boys grow up imitating action heroes, girls are playing with Barbie—a role model they will never be able to successfully emulate because her body proportions are so grossly unrealistic. While boys try to reenact what their role models *do*, girls are busy imitating the way their role models *look*. Men are judged by their accomplishments (or lack thereof), while women are judged by their appearance. Although this double standard has changed some in recent years, too often the new values backfire, with the tragic result that men are now judged also by their appearance and women are judged also by their accomplishments—making it even more difficult for anyone to measure up!

The average North American woman is 5'4" tall and weighs 143 pounds. The average supermodel is 5'11" tall and weighs 117 pounds—meaning that there is a huge discrepancy between what our culture considers ideal and what is, in fact, real. Television, magazines, movies, and billboards all bombard women with this impossible ideal, leaving those who don't fit the mold with the depressing feeling that they are woefully inadequate. In a culture as media-oriented as ours, it is nearly impossible for a woman to escape this pervasive influence.

Sadly, men are now falling prey to the same influence and are becoming more concerned, self-conscious and insecure about their appearance. It's no longer considered enough for men to be successful and powerful, they are also being expected to conform to particular physical standards: to be—and remain—tall, strong, lean and handsome. As a result, they too need reassurance that they don't need a "perfect" body in order to be attractive or lovable. If you are a woman whose husband or boyfriend is being challenged by these issues, Chapter Seven is for you.

Honey, Does This Make My Butt Look Big is a perfect conversation starter. It is filled with scenarios and questions that many couples struggle with in the areas of body image, weight, food, exercise, sexuality, and eating disorders. Each includes a variety of responses, all the way from "doomed to fail" and "missing the point," to "well-meaning" and "good try." Happily, at the end of every scenario is a "winning" response that will get you off the hot seat and preserve (maybe even improve) your relationship.

To each example I have also added a brief insight or bit of advice based on my 20 years of experience in treating these issues, which I offer as a glimpse into the psychology of body image and disordered eating. But please don't assume that they will make you an expert on your honey's process. Ultimately, each person is the only expert on his or her particular situation.

If you find yourself in similar situations, these examples

will give you some ideas for responding more effectively. Better yet, take your understanding one step further and use your own words. There are many ways to say the same thing. Your honey will trust your words more when they are your own and he/she can see that you're sincere. Ultimately, I hope you will learn how to become more honest, empathetic, and supportive partners, especially when faced with these very sensitive subjects.

You will find that although the first six chapters of this book are primarily aimed at women's issues and the seventh at men's, some of the scenarios apply equally well to either gender. Keep this in mind as you read. You can expand your thinking by imagining how you would feel if the roles were reversed, and you were in the other position.

I believe that humor has great healing power, particularly in relationships, so I use it generously throughout the book. However, it is in no way intended to belittle your honey's struggles. No matter how beautiful, thin, brilliant, or successful, very few people in our culture escape these issues. Eating and body image insecurities are at once serious and tragic, frustrating and enraging, frightening and debilitating; and, as this book demonstrates, they can also sometimes seem funny and absurd. So without discounting the seriousness of the problem, have fun reading this book—ideally, together! And, hopefully, you will learn something enlightening and useful about your honey, yourself, and your relationship along the way.

CHAPTER ONE

Image Isn't Everything
Except When She Thinks It Is

It isn't easy being the boyfriend or husband of a woman who is feeling insecure about her appearance. Countless situations arise that can catch you completely off guard and place you in a double bind—damned if you do, damned if you don't. Catch–22. She grapples with these issues and, by voicing her struggles, lures you into their web. It's sticky, intricate, and complex. It's not that she is intentionally trying to ensnare you—she is trying to find answers, solutions, ideas, support, and help.

If you get involved, you may wind up vicariously experiencing the same agony that she struggles with internally. For example, if she gets angry with you, she is probably venting just a fraction of the anger she feels toward herself. If she doubts you, it reflects only a small portion of her own self-doubt. If she believes you when you're lying, it replicates the ways she lies to herself. In other words, your interactions as a couple around these issues become a manifestation of the internal dialogues, arguments, and quandaries that play relentlessly inside her head.

You have only one survival strategy: DON'T GO THERE! It won't help her, and you can't possibly win. Even mental health professionals may be baffled by how to handle these issues. Unless they have very specific education, training, and years of experience treating body image and eating disorders, they too can get caught in the web and become ineffectual or, worse yet, do further damage.

Rather than allowing yourself to be dragged into arbitrating her no-win questions, your job as her partner is simply to love her and make sure she knows it, while protecting yourself and your relationship. So let's take a look at how to do this.

Honey...

Looks Can Be Deceiving

"Does this make me look fat?"

Trouble ahead: *"Well, yes."*

Even if you didn't think she *could* look that fat, never say yes! She'll hate you for being so brutally honest, and she'll hate herself for how she looks.

Futile: *"You're not fat."*

She's not asking if she *is* fat—she's asking if she *looks* fat.

Unproductive: *"I don't know."*

She won't be satisfied with that. Either she'll think it's the cowardly way of telling her she does look fat, or she'll start bombarding you with more (similar) questions that can only get you more deeply entangled.

Good try: *"No."*

If *she* thinks she looks fat, she won't believe you, or she'll think you're just trying to avoid the issue.

Try this instead: *"Honey, you are beautiful and I want you to wear whatever **you** feel good in."*

The Bottom Line

Whenever she asks you about her appearance, size, weight, shape, or body, she is really looking for assurance that she is OK. Every day women are bombarded with messages that anything other than a "perfect" body is a mortal sin, a hopeless failure, and a crime punishable by ostracism, disrespect, and disdain. Under these conditions, it is very hard to hold on to one's self-esteem. So you can help by seizing every opportunity to combat those messages with affirmations of her attractiveness, desirability, and worth—no matter what her size—even if she refutes them.

Also, dignifying the above question with either a yes or no implies that having a large body is an inherently bad thing. We, as a culture, have created this value and now use it to ruthlessly measure not only our own self-worth, but that of others as well. But fat is just a size. We are brainwashed to have judgments and fears about it, but human bodies come in all sizes and shapes. The sooner we accept this truth, the better off we'll be.

Double Trouble

"Which of these outfits do I look better in?"

Unkind: *"Who cares? No one's going to look at you anyway."*
That's downright mean.

Won't fly: *"This one."*
She'll wonder what's wrong with the other one and then pester you for an answer that could lead to trouble.

Good try: *"They're both great."*
If she's willing to let it go that easily…

Try this instead: *"They're both nice. Wear whichever one you feel better in."*

The Bottom Line

This is usually a no-win situation, and you're best off not getting involved. If you tell her you prefer one to the other, she may infer that the other one doesn't look good on her and she might never wear it again. She may also feel embarrassed that she's worn it so many times without realizing that it didn't look good on her. Then she'll be mad at you for not telling her sooner (even if that's not what you meant). Many women feel so harshly judged by their appearance that they are hypersensitive to even the smallest hint of disapproval. You will need to hold a firm boundary when she asks questions like this in order to avoid conflict and hurting her. If she presses the matter, you can be blunt and tell her you know this is risky business and you don't want to get involved in it.

Truth or Dare

She catches you glancing at a sexy bombshell walking by or ogling a babe in a magazine. She says: "I'll bet you wish I looked like her."

Not thinking with your head: *"Oh, yeah!"*

She'll feel ugly and inferior. And you'll be sleeping on the couch.

Well-meaning: *"No."*

Not quite enough of an answer—she probably won't let you leave it at that.

Good try: *"Well, let me put it this way: I may want a Jaguar, but I hear they break down easily, parts are expensive, and they spend a lot of time in the shop. The same could be said about a woman who looks like her. So my answer is 'No.'"*

You get points for the humor, but women do not like to be thought of as objects.

Try this instead: *"If you looked like her, then you wouldn't be you. And it's you I love, just the way you are."*

The Bottom Line

Very few women ever feel satisfied with their bodies or their appearance. In fact, girls experience a dramatic drop in self-esteem when they reach puberty and their bodies begin to change. While boys at that age take pride in the way their own physical changes are making them more manly, girls often perceive themselves as becoming fat instead of becoming womanly. In addition, both boys and girls are influenced by unrealistic media images of what makes a woman attractive and desirable. To counter these messages, it is important that both men and women outspokenly resist the notion that there is only one standard of beauty. Beauty comes in all sizes, shapes, colors, and ages. As a man, you can play an integral role in supporting this principle by frequently expressing appreciation for your honey's body, just the way it is. But also remind her that she is so much more than her body by complementing *all* the qualities—such as intelligence, integrity, creativity, and resourcefulness—that you love about her.

Pick a Number, Any Number

Three or four different sizes of her clothes crowd the closet, yet she still exclaims, "I have nothing to wear!"

Confrontational: *"Are you nuts? The closet is overflowing!"*

In this case, "I have nothing to wear" is more a figure of speech than a literal statement. But read on, and you'll see why it might be true.

Imposing: *"I'll pick something out for you."*

Unless you're a professional stylist or you know which of her clothes currently fit her as well as all the other criteria she's using to select an outfit, it will be much easier to let her grapple with this on her own.

Try this instead: *"Maybe it's time to clean out your closet and go shopping."*

The Bottom Line

Absurd as it might seem, she may actually be telling you the truth. If her weight tends to fluctuate, it's very hard to keep appropriate clothing (that she actually likes and feels comfortable in) for every occasion in all the sizes she wears. She may even own quite a few things that she doesn't really like, but bought because they were the only clothes that fit. And she's reluctant to get rid of clothes that are too small because she's hoping to fit into them again. She also may not be ready to get rid of clothes that are too large, for fear that she'll gain weight and need them again. Even the clothes that do fit may have gone out of style since she was last her current size. So, is it getting easier to see how it's possible to have a closet full of clothes and still have "nothing to wear?"

Does She or Doesn't She?

"Quick! Look! See that woman over there? Am I as fat as she is?"

Better go buy flowers: *"Yes!"*

Clearly she isn't complimenting the woman, so saying yes will be perceived as an insult.

Ineffective: *"No."*

That might not be the end of it. It could prompt more uncomfortable questions such as: How much fatter is she? Does she have similar proportions? Are my arms that flabby? and so on.

Counterproductive: *"She's fatter on the top, and you're fatter on the bottom" (or some variation on that theme).*

She'll feel bad about herself if you say that any part of her is as fat or fatter.

Good try: *"Yes, but you're much more attractive."*

Try this instead: *"I don't compare you to other women, and I wish you wouldn't either."*

The Bottom Line

She may want to know how others see her, or she may be looking for reassurance that she's not *that* fat. In either case, it's far more important that she learn to love and accept herself just as she is. Comparing herself to others only fosters a better-than/worse-than mentality rather than the development of healthy self-esteem. It is an exercise in futility because we are all unique individuals and should be celebrating our differences rather than competing!

Perfectly Unnatural

"I'm thinking of getting a boob job, nose job, eye lift, butt lift, tummy tuck, and/or liposuction..."

Asking for it: *"That's a great idea!"*

She'll see this as an admission that there is something wrong with her body.

Harsh: *"Don't be absurd!"*

She'll assume that you're standing in the way of her having a perfect body, and that you might even feel threatened if she looked better.

Good try: *"You don't need that."*

Only she knows what she really needs.

Right Response: *"It's your body, so it's your decision, but I love you just as you are and would hate to see you undergo a painful and potentially dangerous surgical procedure. Let's talk about it."*

The Bottom Line

Like all surgical procedures, plastic surgery involves health risks and stress to the body and psyche. It also carries an additional risk: your honey may be unhappy with the results, especially if she's trying to find an external solution to an internal problem. She may think that altering her body is the solution to a poor body image, and this can help some people tremendously. But others endure expensive, painful procedures only to discover that body image issues are much too complex to be solved by changing a body part. Another risk is that plastic surgery can become addictive and she could get caught up in an endless and unattainable pursuit of "perfection." She may have an illness called body dysmorphic disorder, a distressing preoccupation or obsession with an imagined or slight defect in one's appearance (see *Resources*). This can be a debilitating condition which requires professional help.

Your Money or Your Wife

"I just can't go to your boss's pool party. I'm much too embarrassed to wear a swimsuit."

Missing the point: *"Nobody cares what you look like."*

This may be true. But it's quite apparent by her statement that *she* cares.

Still missing the point: *"But you **have** to come! It's important for my job that we schmooze with the boss and his wife."*

No doubt this is true, too, but you're overlooking her distress about her appearance.

Dismissive: *"Don't be ridiculous. You look fine."*

No one likes their feelings to be called ridiculous. They're not ridiculous to her, or you wouldn't be having this conversation.

Try this instead: *"You don't have to wear a swimsuit. Wear whatever you feel good in. It's important to me that you come with me and that you feel comfortable being there."*

The Bottom Line

Here you have yet another glimpse at how tortured women can be by beliefs about their appearance. Some will even pass up social events and physical activities and miss out on the pleasures of life because they are afraid of being judged or ridiculed about their appearance (which does happen). Making peace with their bodies is an enormous challenge. So honor this challenge by listening to your honey's feelings and being compassionate even though you may not fully understand. At social events where she may feel uncomfortable, you can make a big difference. Subtle displays of affection such as holding her hand, taking her by the arm, or placing your arm lightly around her are extremely reassuring. They also make a public statement that you love this woman and are proud to let others know it.

Sun Bunny to Love

She regularly goes to a tanning salon or tans herself in the midday sun without sunscreen because she thinks a tan makes her look thinner.

Watch out: *"A tan won't make you look thinner, it will just make your fat darker."*

Nobody likes their fat talked about.

Condescending: *"Haven't you heard of skin cancer?"*

Unless she's illiterate, of course she has. But her poor body image is winning out over her health.

Try this instead: *"I'm afraid that you might get skin cancer. Would you be willing to try some of the new tanning lotions or a spray tanning salon instead? Even supermodels are using them now."*

The Bottom Line

There is a name for this condition: tanorexia. Derived from the word anorexia, it refers to the obsession with or addiction to tanning. In many cases, women tan excessively because they erroneously believe that a darker body, like darker clothes, makes them look slimmer. This can also be a symptom of more serious body image distortions. Whatever the cause, this practice puts women at high risk for skin cancer. Tanning outdoors exposes people to higher degrees of ultraviolet radiation due to recent depletion of the earth's protective ozone layer. Tanning salons have also been found to increase chances of dangerous cancers by seven times, and injuries from tanning salons (especially to the eyes) are on the rise. I can't help wondering why we ever stopped using parasols!

Mirror, Mirror on the Wall

She looks in the mirror, grabs parts of her body, and exclaims, "I hate myself!"

Heartless: *Say nothing.*
She'll feel invisible or ignored.

Reprimanding: *"Oh, stop it!"*
She'll feel chastised and dismissed.

Good try: *"Don't be silly."*
She'll feel that you're not taking her seriously.

Try this: *Go to her and gently put your arms around her. Tell her you wish she could see herself through your eyes, for then she would know how beautiful she is.*

The Bottom Line

How is it that your honey could hate herself so much, you wonder? Because she lives in a culture that tolerates nothing less than perfection in women's bodies and she's confronted with this message daily. At a deeper level, if she has not developed a sense of self-esteem and self-worth beyond her looks, or she feels disappointed with herself in other ways, she may blame her body. Intense body hatred can also be a symptom of physical or sexual abuse. Even if she doesn't recall such abuse, the possibility could warrant further exploration. Explore the possibility of body dysmorphic disorder as well.

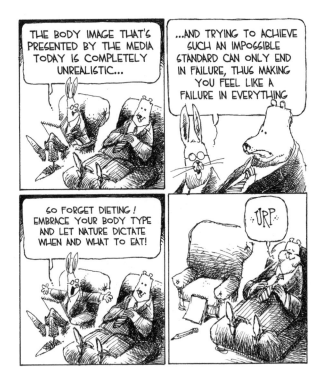

CHAPTER TWO

To Eat or Not to Eat:
When Food Isn't a Piece of Cake

Food. It seems like a simple enough word, yet it represents something that is absolutely essential for our survival. It plays a central role in celebrations and rituals, and the sight, smell, or taste of it can conjure up memories or associations with distant events or people. Food can be an expression of love (ask any Jewish or Italian mother, or visit a candy store on Valentine's Day), and a weapon in political embargoes.

Although many people see it as merely something to eat, food is actually one of the most significant and powerful forces in our lives. At the very least, our bodies demand it every day. Additionally, we may be required to shop for it, store it, prepare it, or select it from a menu. For millions of women, however, every one of these encounters with food can feel like a fight—from a small skirmish to a full-fledged battle riddled with painful emotions. For the woman who struggles with eating and body image issues, food can be the bane of her existence.

Further complicating matters is the fact that many women are apt to distinguish between foods that they consider "good" and "bad" depending on current dieting fads, and they will judge themselves good or bad for eating them. Even the guidelines for what actually constitutes "healthy" food and "normal" eating seem to change as often as the weather!

In more serious cases, a relationship with a woman who has food issues can even take on a dynamic similar to that of an alcoholic and their significant other (also known as a co-alcoholic or codependent). Like the alcoholic's spouse, you will discover that you cannot control or change how your honey feels about food. As a man, you have probably been trained to "fix things," but you definitely can't fix this one for her. You must remain detached no matter how hard she may try to lure you in, and keep your focus on taking care of yourself and the relationship.

In this chapter you will read some typical interactions you may experience with your honey in situations that involve food. As you consider these, keep in mind that she is a competent, capable, intelligent woman and deserves to be treated as such. When it comes to food and her body image, though, she may seem a bit nutty! But she is also the victim of an entire culture's confusion and conflict about what, when, where, and how much to eat. So be patient with her, and with yourself, as you learn a new way of responding.

Honey...

Fettuccine vs. Spinach

"Should I get the fettuccine alfredo or the spinach salad?"

Bound to backfire: *"The spinach salad."*

She'll think you're implying that she needs to lose weight or that you want to deprive her of pleasure.

Also bound to backfire: *"The fettuccine alfredo."*

Not unless you want to be accused of sabotaging her and trying to make her fat.

Good try: *"Well, that depends on whether or not you're on your diet tonight."*

This can easily be misconstrued as a judgment and sounds oh-so-very condescending.

Try this instead: *"Whichever you prefer, Honey."*

Food for Thought

You're being lured into an inner battle that has no foreseeable positive outcome. Sometimes, winning means choosing the fettuccine, thereby asserting her autonomy over everyone who has ever told her she has to be thin to be lovable. At other times, winning means choosing something healthy because she wants to care for herself. The battle is a complex one with many undercover spies, traitors, and saboteurs at war inside of her. Save yourself, stay out of it altogether and let her decide.

Harm's Way

"If you see me eating something I shouldn't, will you please stop me?"

Hazardous: *"Yes."*

If you value your relationship and your life, *never* get between a woman and her food!

Pointless: *"Like what, for instance?"*

You don't even *want* to know what she "shouldn't" be eating because it will set you up to become her food police, a dangerous and thankless job.

Good try: *"Only if it's poisonous!"*

This is actually a great response because it indicates that you already know not to get involved in her food choices, and that you have a sense of humor about it. However, she will probably need more of an explanation to understand that the best way to support her is to respect her autonomy.

Try this instead: *"No, because I don't want to control you and I don't want you to feel controlled by me."*

Food for Thought

She's feeling insecure about her ability to care for herself and make healthy choices, so she's relinquishing her power and asking you to do it for her. If you do, you both lose. It's impossible for you to know the best choice for her at any given time. Only she can know that. If you become her food monitor, she will end up resenting you and sneaking or hiding food from you. In addition, she won't learn to trust her own judgment and will remain disempowered. Your best course is to refuse any kind of participation in her food choices. Just continue to love and support her in making her own decisions.

Buyer's Remorse

"I shouldn't have eaten that."

Confrontational: *"Then why did you?"*

Asking her to explain her actions may put her on the defensive. Besides, she might not even know why she did it.

Uncaring: *"You're right. You shouldn't have."*

She has already expressed remorse. Agreeing with her will only rub it in and make her feel worse.

Presumptuous: *"I could have told you that."*

No matter how well you know her, it really isn't possible for you to know when or what she should or shouldn't eat. Her decisions about food are more complex than they appear on the surface.

Good try: *"It's OK, just this once won't matter."*

You're right about this. Once doesn't matter, but it's probably not just this once that she's regretting.

Try this instead: *If you can relate, tell her you know the feeling. If you can't, look lovingly into her eyes and simply touch her hand or put your arm around her.*

Food for Thought

Because food is a struggle for her, many factors affect her decisions about whether and what to eat. What might seem obvious to you as her most sensible choice may be viewed differently from her perspective. Because situations differ, she can't always know in advance how she'll feel afterward. Sometimes she may consciously decide she really wants something only to discover it wasn't as good as she thought it would be. Other times, the compulsion to eat just takes over and she makes an irrational choice. So whenever your honey feels like she has made a mistake with food, treat her as you would treat anyone who has regrets: with compassion, understanding and support.

How Sweet It Isn't

"Should I order dessert?"

Think twice: *"Sure."*

If she orders dessert and feels guilty after eating it, you become an easy target to blame.

Pushing it: *"I don't **think** so."*

However supportive your intentions might be, telling her not to eat something will not make her happy.

Good try: *"What **kind** of dessert? Cheesecake or a fruit cup?"*

Had she just wanted a fruit cup, she wouldn't have bothered to ask your opinion!

Try this instead: *"That's entirely up to you, Honey."*

Food for Thought

She doesn't *really* want your opinion about dessert. She's just giving voice to one small aspect of an internal debate that may have been triggered by the dessert menu, but probably began long before you met her. It's a debate between two parts of herself that are very divided: one thinks she has to diet constantly to be "good;" the other believes she should be able to eat whatever she wants, whenever she wants. You don't want to take sides on this, because it will only complicate her struggle, and she may shift her frustration onto you. Loving her means loving all of her and empowering her to make her own choices about food—whatever they are.

Desserts Is "Stressed" Spelled Backward

The waiter has just delivered your favorite dessert. Before you've even touched it, she says, "Can I have a bite?"

On shaky ground: *"Well, if you **really** want one..."*

She'll feel judged and think you're being smug and condescending.

Alienating: *"No."*

She'll feel humiliated and think you're saying she doesn't *need* it.

Good try: *"OK, but just **one** bite."*

Again she'll feel humiliated and think you're saying she doesn't need it, and in addition, that you're being stingy.

Try this instead: *"Of course."*

Food for Thought

Never deny her food, even if you know she'll eat more of your dessert than you will! You can always order another. One of the major origins of women's eating problems is deprivation—the withholding of love, attention, affection, and sometimes food or certain types of food. As a consequence, food becomes a substitute or compensation for what was, or is, missing in their lives. Not sharing food with her can reactivate these feelings of deprivation and be misinterpreted as withholding not only food, but also your love. So be generous with her always and in all ways. If you want to avoid the whole matter altogether, next time don't order dessert!

Psychological Thriller

At the movie theater she suddenly reaches over and starts eating your buttered popcorn.

Insolent: *You slap her hand away.*

Whoa! That smacks of a parent-child relationship (not a very healthy one), and it's horribly demeaning.

Humiliating: *"Do you really think you should?"*

Who made *you* her conscience?

Stating the obvious: *"But it's got butter on it..."*

Of course it does! That's what makes it appealing. If it didn't, she probably wouldn't bother with it!

Try this instead: *Put it in the middle where you both can reach it.*

Food for Thought

You've probably noticed a theme by now. *Never* try to stop her from eating. *Never* comment on what or why she is eating. *Never* deny or refuse her food. Just stay out of it! Ultimately, you'll both be a lot happier if you do.

Pizza My Heart

"I want to celebrate my weight loss. Let's go out for pizza and ice cream!"

Arrogant: *"That doesn't make any sense!"*

Maybe not to you, but it does to her. This is her call, let her make it.

Controlling: *"No!"*

If you're saying no because you don't think she should be eating pizza and ice cream, think again! You're trying to control her eating.

Good try: *"OK, but how about going for a run first?"*

Examine your motives! Are you suggesting running as a way to compensate for the calories she'll be consuming?

Try this instead: *"OK. When do you want to go?"*

Food for Thought

Pizza and ice cream to celebrate weight loss may seem contradictory, but not to the woman who has endured a restrictive diet for any length of time. Eating a moderate amount of such foods on occasion will not undermine her progress. In fact, the sense of deprivation that ensues when foods are *forbidden* is far more harmful. (Remember Eve and the forbidden apple?) Deprivation is often the prelude to bingeing and other self-destructive behavior. Regardless of your well-meaning inclination to "help," decisions affecting her body are hers to make.

Her Stash

You discover a bag of junk food hidden under her side of the bed.

Gloating: Say, *"Aha! Look what I found!"*

You're not hunting for Easter eggs! She hid it because she didn't want you to see it.

Ineffective: *Put it on top of the bed.*

This will only serve to shame her and force her to find another hiding spot!

Impulsive: *Eat it yourself.*

She will feel ashamed at having her secret discovered, angry that you took what belonged to her, and doubly angry that you can eat that junk without the same consequences she experiences.

Good try: *Put it in the pantry.*

Despite the covert message that she doesn't have to hide or sneak food from you, she'll still be embarrassed.

Try this instead: *Do nothing.*

Food for Thought

A hidden stash of food may be an old habit acquired from past situations when her eating was criticized or controlled by others. Busting her on her stash can trigger those old feelings and make you the bad guy (despite your good intentions). Her stash may represent her need for autonomy and independence. Until she can find and access her own personal power in other ways, it may be important for her to keep her stash. Don't take her food away. You might inadvertently be taking a lot more than just food.

Your Stash

You discover that your own secret bag of junk food has vanished without a trace.

Shaming: *Assume she ate it and confront her.*

If she ate it, it's gone and you can't have it back. So are you just trying to make her feel bad?

Subversive: *Stock the house with all her favorite junk food so she'll leave yours alone.*

Remember that this is the woman you love. And while revenge may seem sweet, sabotaging her well-being is not.

Good try: *Get another stash and lock it up this time.*

If you're so adamant about keeping junk food in the house, perhaps you should examine your own relationship to food.

Try this instead: *Be a love and don't keep it in the house!*

Food for Thought

By now you probably realize that she has an unusual relationship to food. She can't just take it or leave it. It calls to her like the legendary sirens that lured sailors to their death. Living in a society where food is so abundant and omnipresent poses a tremendous challenge for her. Home should be a place of safety, serenity, and sanctuary. If she prefers to keep certain overly tempting foods out of the house, you can help by respecting that choice. You can always eat whatever you want outside the house.

Let Them Eat Cake

You're at a birthday party together, and she declines a piece of birthday cake.

Meddlesome: *"Aw, come on, one little piece won't hurt."*
Why are you pushing food on her?

Well-intentioned: *"Atta girl!"*
She doesn't want attention called to what she eats or doesn't eat. Just stay out of her food!

Try this instead: *Don't say or do anything at all.*

Food for Thought

If your response is, "One little piece won't hurt," you should give serious thought to why you are pushing food on her. Are you concerned that if she loses weight, she'll attract more male attention? Has her weight given you a false sense of security about the relationship? Are you afraid of losing an eating partner? If she decides to eat more healthfully, will you be forced to examine your own food choices? Do you feel threatened by the changes she is making both externally and internally? Be aware of what's going on inside you if you bring home junk food that you know she's trying to avoid. Be brutally honest in examining your motives. And don't be afraid to discuss your fears with her. She would much rather hear that you are afraid of losing her than think you are trying to sabotage her efforts. Always avoid making comments in public about what she eats or doesn't eat. Remember, when it comes to her relationship with food, just don't go there!

Busted

You come home unexpectedly early and find her polishing off an entire cheesecake.

Shaming: *"I can't believe you're eating all that!"*
Get over it—and fast. She doesn't need your judgment.

Intrusive: *"I hope that's a nonfat, sugar-free, low-carb cheesecake!"*
If she says, "Yes, and it tastes great!" call me immediately and tell me where I can get one!

Good try: *"I worry about you when I see you eating that much unhealthy food."*

Try this instead: *Give her a kiss on the cheek and say, "Is everything OK?"*

Food for Thought

You've caught her red-handed in the middle of a binge, but there's no need to be alarmed. Lots of people binge occasionally with no serious consequences. But evidence that this is a frequent occurrence warrants a serious discussion, because she may have binge eating disorder or bulimia (see Chapter Six). Talk to her in a non-confrontational and nonjudgmental manner; otherwise, she may become defensive, angry, or more secretive.

CHAPTER THREE

I'm Too Sexy for My Body

When Baring It All Is Too Much to Bear

Being naked in front of someone else, particularly someone we want to impress, can be difficult at the best of times. We feel exposed and vulnerable, unable to hide or camouflage our physical "flaws." Most people have dreamt of finding themselves naked or only partially clothed in a public place and feeling intense embarrassment. These dreams usually reflect our hidden fear, anxiety, and shame. For the woman with body image issues, being seen naked can be a *real* nightmare.

We are exposed daily to media riddled with perfected images of models and celebrities. Magazines, newspapers, billboards, TV, and movies all reinforce the belief that for a woman to be attractive and successful, she must resemble these ideal images. Less apparent, however, is the work involved in creating this artificial appearance. Many models and celebrities follow rigid, restrictive diets and strenuous exercise routines. Many even suffer from eating disorders. They spend countless hours of discomfort under the hands of professional make-up artists, hairdressers, and plastic surgeons. Their breasts are taped up, their butts are squeezed into body shapers, and their flaws are air-brushed away. If all else fails, a body double is sometimes used. Supermodel Cindy Crawford once said, "Even I don't wake up looking like Cindy Crawford."

Real bodies—real women—do *not* look like the women in fashion magazines. We have blemishes, cellulite, birthmarks, and moles. We are fat and thin, short and tall, and every shape in the fruit basket, from pears to apples to bananas. We have breasts that are barely there or so big that they hurt our backs, butts of infinite variety, and hair in places that some men didn't even know was possible. And as we age, bear children, endure illnesses or surgeries, we acquire wrinkles, stretch marks, scars, and sagging eyelids, necks, breasts, and stomachs. The female cultural ideal is merely an illusion.

Yet every day, women waste precious life energy feeling ashamed of their bodies or desperately trying to change them into something nature never intended them to be. The challenge for all of us is to expand our definition of beauty to include women of all sizes, shapes, colors, and ages. We need to learn genuine appreciation for the amazing diversity of the human body.

Your task is to reassure your Honey that you love her just the way she is, "warts and all," and that changing her body is not going to change the way you feel about her. This sentiment is summed up perfectly by the following anonymous quote: "You don't love a woman because she is beautiful; she is beautiful because you love her."

Honey...

Modern Version of a Headache

"Not tonight, Honey... I feel too fat."

Missing the point: *"You're not fat!"*
The issue is not her size, it's how she feels!

Self-centered: *"Aw, c'mon, Honey... please?"*
Trust me, this is not very seductive or enticing. It's selfish (not to mention desperate). And it addresses only your need, not hers.

Good try: *"But Honey, you know I don't care!"*
What exactly is it that you don't care about? How fat she is, or how she feels?

Try this instead: *"Is it really your body that's bothering you, or is there something else?"*

The Naked Truth

Fat is not a feeling. She may be feeling bloated or full from water retention or a big meal, but "feeling fat" is a state of mind that reflects underlying emotional issues. If she is unaccustomed to identifying her feelings and expressing them in a healthy manner, she may unconsciously channel them into body hatred. For example, she may be angry at someone whom she doesn't feel safe confronting, so she directs that anger at herself instead. And a vulnerability about her weight or body image issues is a familiar place for unresolved emotions to roost. Encouraging her to talk about what's really going on is your best means of offering support when you hear those three little words, "I feel fat."

Lights Out

Whenever you become sexual, she insists on turning off the light.

Counterproductive: *Insist on keeping the light on.*

That will only lead to a power struggle, and it could kill the mood!

Doomed to fail: *Wait till things get hot and heavy, then switch the light back on.*

That will definitely kill the mood—and piss her off.

Good try: *Initiate sex during daylight.*

If you're seductive enough, this could actually work!

Try this instead: *Offer to dim the lights very low or, even better, to light a candle.*

The Naked Truth

She's making it very clear that she is uncomfortable being seen during physical intimacy. This could be because she feels modest or self-conscious about her body. It could also be that being so vulnerable and exposed feels too intense for her. She may be able to let go more easily if she doesn't see you seeing her. She may also have inhibitions about sex that are easier to overcome if she doesn't see what's happening. Whatever her reasons, be gentle and patient with her. Later, you can tell her you're interested in knowing why she wants the lights out, and reassure her that you won't turn up the dimmer until she's ready.

Hot Mama

She's pregnant and says: "Honey, I'm miserable. I don't feel sexy at all. I feel and look like a cow!"

Sweet but misguided: *"Well, I think you look like a very sexy cow."*

Unless you want to sleep alone for the rest of your lives together, under no circumstances should you ever refer to her as a cow!

Uncouth: *"You don't look like a cow. But that woman in our birthing class? She looks like a cow!"*

Be nice! And don't encourage comparisons, they're counterproductive.

Good try: *"Don't worry, Honey. You'll lose the weight after you've had the baby."*

That doesn't address the way she's feeling now. And weight loss is not really the issue here.

Try this instead: *"I'm sorry you're feeling so bad. I think you look more beautiful than ever."*

Or better yet: *Make like a bull and charge at her!*

The Naked Truth

Pregnancy causes such radical changes in such a short period of time that it can trigger all kinds of physical and emotional discomfort. She has to endure: mood swings from hormonal changes, morning sickness, swollen feet, an aching back, clothes that don't fit, trouble bending over, and being kicked from the inside. Perhaps most challenging of all, she has to adapt to a body that is constantly going through changes over which she has absolutely no control. She needs you to regularly remind her how beautiful she is, demonstrate your desire for her, give her frequent foot and back rubs, and thank her for carrying your baby.

The Forbidden Zone

She never lets you touch her _____ even during your most intimate moments.

Invasive: *Touch her there anyway.*
It's her body, and she gets to call the shots!

Clueless: *"Your fat doesn't bother me."*
Don't refer to her fat while being intimate—it carries too much charge.

Good try: *"But I like to touch your _____."*
What's important is whether or not *she* likes to be touched there.

Try this instead: *"I look forward to the day when you love your body as much as I do, and I'll be able to touch you all over!"*

The Naked Truth

When a woman doesn't want you to touch her in a particular place, most likely it's because she feels there is something wrong with that part of her body. By touching her there, you call attention to it. She then becomes self-conscious and afraid that you will judge it as harshly as she does, no matter how strongly you disagree. Until she feels better about her body, it's best to respect her boundaries. You could, however, ask if she's willing to try some desensitization techniques by letting you touch her there for a brief moment and then slowly and gradually increasing the time as she learns to relax and enjoy it. This may help her grow accustomed to the sensation. It may also be healing for her to have a loving hand touch the parts that she has not been able to love herself. But first and foremost, be sure to honor any limits she sets about her body.

Ass Backwards

Whenever she's naked, she has an odd habit of walking around backwards.

Naive: *Assume it's a neurological problem.*

   Your first clue that it's not neurological is that she only does it when she's naked!

Disrespectful: *Sneak up behind her.*

   You might want to find out what's going on first!

Try this instead: *"Honey, why do you walk around backwards whenever you're naked?"*

Or this: *Just ignore it.*

The Naked Truth

When you don't understand her, sometimes the easiest thing to do is also the most obvious: just ask. Then again, in this case, you don't have to be Freud to figure out that she doesn't want you to see her naked backside! Once she knows you're on to this, she'll probably feel ridiculous continuing to walk around backwards. At that point she may just give up the charade or choose to cover up with a towel or robe. Eventually, she will probably tire of trying to hide her body and stop. It's sometimes true that if you ignore a problem long enough, it will go away by itself.

Barely There

She will make love in only one position because she's too self-conscious of her body in other positions.

Blaming response: *"This is getting boring."*

She'll feel guilty and pressured—feelings which are never a good prelude to intimacy.

Well-meaning: *"I already know what you look like, so what difference does it make?"*

It may not make a difference to you, but to her this is an entirely different realm.

Try this instead: *"Is there anything I can do to help you feel more comfortable?"*

The Naked Truth

Trying new positions increases her feelings of exposure, vulnerability, and risk. It may give you vantage points of her body that she herself has never had. It can expose you to smells and tastes that she may feel insecure about and is afraid you won't find pleasing. Continuing to do what's familiar and comfortable is much easier.

To help ease her out of her comfort zone, together you could look at books or videos which tastefully and respectfully introduce new ideas about physical intimacy (see *Resources*). Some address positions and techniques, while others explore deeper intimacy and soulful connection through sex. Be patient. She needs to know that you will honor her boundaries, that she can trust you, and that you won't shame her. This is usually a gradual process. But sometimes when a woman catches on to what she's been missing, she can become a very eager and enthusiastic lover. Beware of what you might awaken; you might have to build up your stamina and endurance just to keep up with her!

CHAPTER FOUR

Weighty Matters:
When Size Does Matter

In 1997, a landmark study on body image published in *Psychology Today* revealed that an astounding 89 percent of women want to lose weight and that, horrifyingly, 15 percent would sacrifice more than five years of their lives to attain their goal weight. These sad statistics clearly reveal how damaging the concept of an ideal weight can be—it is one of the most harmful influences on a woman's self-esteem. If a woman believes she is overweight, her feelings of worthlessness will discount all her other accomplishments, no matter how impressive they may be. Think about Oprah Winfrey: overcoming extreme poverty, physical and sexual abuse, and racial and gender oppression, she became the wealthiest self-made woman in the world. Yet when once asked what she considered her single greatest achievement in life, Oprah answered, "Losing weight."

Many women weigh themselves every day and allow the numbers on the scale to dictate their mood and behavior for the entire day. If the numbers seem too high, they become depressed, irritable, unproductive, asexual, and filled with self-loathing. Or, if they are pleased with the numbers, they feel proud, powerful, and confident—all emotions that shouldn't depend on their weight. The greatest irony is that there is no such thing as an "ideal weight" that would apply to everyone, whether grouped by height, age, bone structure, or any other criteria. Even the term *overweight* is absurd— over what weight? Says who?

The dictionary defines overweight as "weighing more than is allowed, proper, or healthful." Yet the most commonly used weight tables are not scientifically sound, and abundant research contradicts the belief that being heavy is inherently a health hazard. Being *unfit*, not *fat*, is what's unhealthy. In fact, it is possible to be both fat and fit. According to Dr. Glenn Gaesser, author of *Big Fat Lies*, fat people who exercise regularly have a lower risk of premature death than thin people who don't exercise. So much for the ultimate weapon that fat-phobics like to employ: "I'm concerned about your health."

Ironically, at a time when women are enjoying greater equality with men, exciting new career and educational opportunities, and expanding lifestyle choices, we continue to see an ever-growing obsession with their body size, shape, and weight, beginning as early as age five. Theories abound as to the cause of this obsession, how, when and why it began, and who is responsible—none of which can be proven. I'd like to encourage everyone, men and women alike to take personal responsibility for this obsession. Though we may not be able to change the dominant cultural idea of beauty, individually we can each begin to challenge our own belief systems.

There is great truth in the old adage, "Beauty is in the eye of the beholder" because beauty is neither a universal nor a timeless concept. A review of the fleeting feminine ideal over time reveals that in the late 19th century, Peter Paul Rubens painted his era's beauties as soft, round, and voluptuous, while in the Roaring '20s, flappers strapped their breasts flat in order to look thinner. In the 1950s the zaftig, curvaceous Marilyn Monroe became an enduring sex symbol, while only about 10 years later, the 1960s produced Twiggy, who made looking anorexic seem fashionable.

It is important to evaluate our ideas about beauty and realize the extent to which they are influenced by our culture. However, this is no easy feat. Weight and size are numbers that are vested with disproportionate power and can be incredibly deceptive. Many men are shocked to learn that a woman they consider attractive or sexy wears a size 18 or weighs 170 pounds. And a great number of men actually prefer women who are full-figured, ample-bodied or fat. Yet their numbers remain largely unknown because so many have learned to be ashamed of their feelings.

The real challenge we face is to recognize that weight bias is nothing more than another form of prejudice. No woman, no matter how thin or fat, should suffer oppression, discrimination, or criticism because of her size or weight—from others or herself and especially not from the man who loves her most. As her partner, you can play an important role in helping free your honey from food, weight and body image issues. However, you can only fulfill this role if you are able to rise above society's insidious love/hate affair with physical appearance.

Honey...

Weight Wise

"Do you think I need to lose weight?"

Sleeping on the couch tonight: *"You could stand to lose a few pounds."*

That may sound harmless to you, but she's probably hypersensitive about her weight, and this will only make her more so.

Crude: *"Just in your lower half, don't lose any on top!"*

A reply like this fosters self-consciousness about various parts of her body. Women want to be seen as people, not parts!

Good try: *"You may not need to, but you might want to."*

Technically this may be true, but what she'll hear is that *you* want her to lose weight.

Try this instead: *"That's up to you. I love you just the way you are."*

The Real Skinny

This can be a very loaded and confusing question. It's her body, her life, and her decision whether or not to lose weight. So why is she asking you? She's probably looking for help in countering a culture and an inner voice that tell her she can never be too thin and that her worth is determined by her weight. Be careful here, it's easy to unintentionally join sides with forces that are constantly undermining her self-esteem. And once you're there, it's hard to switch sides. She needs reassurance that she is beautiful and lovable no matter how much she weighs.

Diet Is a 4-Letter Word

"Honey, will you go on a diet with me?"

Too Hasty: *"Sure."*

Do you know what kind of diet you've just agreed to go on with her? The Atkins Diet? The Zone Diet? The McDougall Diet? The grapefruit diet? The vegetable soup diet? Low-fat, high-carb diet? High-protein, low-carb diet? Jenny Craig? Weight Watchers? Do you have any idea what you're getting into?

Intolerant: *"Oh no, not again."*

Get used to it. Until she finds a lasting solution, she may try dieting on and off for the rest of your lives.

Good try: *"You **know** that diets don't work."*

While this may be true all but two percent of the time, hope runs eternal and she really wants to be part of that two percent.

Try this instead: *"No, I don't want to go on a diet, but I'll support you any way I can, as long as what you do is healthy and balanced."*

The Real Skinny

There are inherent risks in trying to be supportive by dieting with her. Although the two of you may influence one another in a positive way, the opposite is just as likely to happen. For example, if you decide to "cheat," she may feel justified in doing the same. If you go off the diet, she may feel betrayed or blame you if she fails. If you are better at sticking to the diet, she may feel inferior or defeated. The most obvious risk, however, is that you will both regain any lost weight once the diet ends. And possibly more! Dieting in the traditional sense of limiting food and caloric intake is an outdated, ineffective concept. Current trends are to focus on health and fitness, not just thinness, and learn to appreciate the strength and beauty of all sizes. So if her diet is a healthy one, try eating similarly without making any commitments. If her diet is an unhealthy one, express your concerns and refuse to support or participate in it. And avoid eating in front of her—or keeping in the house—foods that tempt her. Remember, this is her journey and you can't walk it for her, but you can walk beside her.

Less Is More

"Would you love me more if I were thinner?"

Dangerous: *"It depends on what you mean by love."*
You're headed down the wrong path with that one...

Close but no cigar: *"It wouldn't change how much I love you, but you might look better."*
You've given a confirmation of your love but coupled it with an insult!

Insightful but evasive: *"Would you love yourself more if you were thinner?"*
This is an excellent question but she wants to know how you feel.

Try this instead: *"No, because my love for you has absolutely nothing to do with how much you weigh."*

The Real Skinny

She's feeling insecure: about her appearance, about your feelings for her, about her lovability. Also, women sometimes funnel their insecurities about other situations in their lives onto their body. She may be feeling incompetent at work or inadequate as a mother or wife, and illogically think that losing weight would resolve those problems. You might want to ask her if something besides her weight is fueling this insecurity or if you've done anything that may have triggered it and offer to talk it over with her. Loving her body is difficult enough when there is so much societal pressure to be thin, but this becomes even harder when her body is a repository for countless unresolved feelings and issues. She needs to know that your love is not dependent on her size and that you are available to explore the underlying issues of her body hatred. This kind of unconditional love, acceptance and support is one of the greatest gifts you will ever be able to give her.

Lost and Found

She loses weight, then gains it back— plus more.

Temporary insanity: *"Geez, looks like you've gained weight again!"*

I guarantee you that she already knows she's gained weight and doesn't need anyone to tell her.

Destined for the doghouse: *Slap her butt and say, "Getting a little chunky, aren't we?"*

Be very careful when it comes to this sensitive subject. She may just slap you back!

Good try: *"You must be so disappointed to have gained all that weight back."*

Even though this is a supportive and empathetic statement, she may not be ready to hear it.

Try this instead: *Don't say or do anything at all.*

The Real Skinny

Losing weight can be exhilarating for her: clothes fit better or are getting too big. Physical activity becomes easier, and people pay her compliments. By contrast, gaining weight can be devastating: clothes are too tight or don't fit at all. Moving around is more difficult and uncomfortable. She catches people making furtive head-to-toe glances that clearly indicate they've noticed her weight gain. She feels disappointed at best, ashamed at worst and in either case, like a failure. Chances are, her weight will naturally fluctuate throughout her life, and so the absolute best you can offer her is unwavering love. If she's gained weight, don't talk about it unless she does so first. Then, as always, make it clear that you love her just as she is.

Weight Watcher

"Will you help me watch my weight?"

Beware: *"Sure."*

This would be a very big mistake—and I think you already know that!

Sarcastic: *"I already do: I watch it go up and down, over and over again!"*

Very funny, wise guy! But not very nice, is it?

Try this instead: *"Sorry, but I've been reading a really great book that says it's best for both of us if I don't get involved in your weight issues."*

The Real Skinny

Watching her weight is difficult enough for her to do, but it's totally impossible for you to do. At best, you can only help keep your home stocked with healthy food, contribute suggestions about healthy meals to eat together, and perhaps offer a supportive ear if she needs to talk. At worst, however, you would be commenting on whether she looks thinner or fatter, what she eats, when she eats, how much she eats—all recipes for disaster!

Dieting for Dollars

"I'm thinking of joining Diet Program X. It costs $$$ a month. What do you think?"

Too controlling: *"Absolutely not!"*

She'll accuse you of thinking she's not worth it. Then she'll remind you how much you spent on your new set of titanium golf clubs, the endless computer upgrades, or restoring that '69 Mach 1 Mustang that just sits in the garage!

Caution: *"Great idea!"*

The diet industry thrives on failure because diets don't usually work. And some diets pose dangerous health risks.

Good try: *"I don't think that's a very good program. Isn't that the diet so-and-so went on the first time she lost and then regained all that weight?"*

Try this instead: *"Honey, I've read that diets don't work. You might want to consider some other options; but, of course, it's up to you."*

The Real Skinny

Dieting is a $33-billion-per-year industry that succeeds because of people's failures. Ninety-five percent of dieters regain any weight they lost within three years, and 98 percent do so within five years. That's because dieting is at best only a temporary and partial solution. Better to focus on creating a healthier lifestyle, with good eating habits, more whole foods, regular exercise, some honest self-examination and a good support system. In addition, your honey may be fighting genetics by trying to become a size that nature never intended her to be. So she may need to make peace with a body that doesn't fit the cultural ideal. But she has to come to these conclusions on her own and in her own time.

Bibliotherapy

She has a gazillion different books on dieting and eating issues, but keeps buying more.

Cynical: *"Why do you bother? It's a waste of money."*
Maybe so, maybe not. You can't really know this for sure.

Out of touch: *"Can't you just read the ones you have?"*
Some books may be redundant, but others might have new information or a new approach that works better for her.

Good try: *"I don't think the solution is in yet another book. I think it's inside you."*
True enough, but she may need some outside help to find it.

Try this instead: *Leave it alone.*

The Real Skinny

Trying to control her behavior will only cause trouble between you. The only legitimate reason to talk to her about buying so many books would be budgetary constraints, and then you could suggest using the library. Otherwise, your wisest move is to let her seek out her own way, in her own time. With support, she'll be able to find the answers she needs. No one can predict where they will come from so any potential healing resources should not be eliminated. She also needs to know you're on her side, rather than thinking that you're trying to obstruct her process.

Dream On

"Wow! Look at this ad! It says that without changing the way I eat, I can lose weight and build muscle while I sleep! Now that's a plan I could stick to."

Inconsiderate: *"Yeah—in your dreams!"*

Even if she only partly believes the ad, she'll perceive this as flippant and insensitive.

Dismissive: *Roll your eyes and walk away.*

This issue is important to her and you diminish and dismiss it with this type of response.

Logical but cold: *"That's a bunch of bull, and you'd be a fool to fall for it."*

You're completely right on both counts! But this is such a sensitive area that a kinder, gentler approach will be more effective.

Try this instead: *"That's a rather remarkable claim and would be great if it's true. Is there any research to back it up? Do they offer a money-back guarantee?"*

The Real Skinny

It's very difficult to watch an otherwise intelligent and discriminating woman acting so gullible and naive. She is simply giving expression to the part of her that feels hopeless about her situation and is tempted to resort to "magical thinking," that is, the illusion that something outside of herself can "fix" her. So remember that she's not stupid, that she's struggling, and that you love her. Help her see that, unfortunately, some people capitalize on others' vulnerabilities by making fraudulent claims. (For places to report such scams, see *Resources*)

Can't Win for Losing

The last time she swore off dieting, she asked you to hide the scale and promise not to give it back. One day, you come home to a torn-apart house and you hear, "Where the hell did you hide the scale? I have to weigh myself!"

You won't get off that easily: *"I'm not telling!"*

She's already worked up. Don't provoke her further, just get the scale!

Don't go there: *"Why do you have to weigh yourself?"*

Do you really want to know? Forget your promise, and go get the scale!

Good try: *"I gave it to Goodwill."*

Unless you really did, don't lie. She's clearly got enough problems without being deceived.

Try this: *Realize you made a mistake by agreeing to hide the scale, silently vow never to get this over-involved again, and GO GET THE SCALE!*

The Real Skinny

This is a classic example of how "helping" can backfire. No matter how good your intentions, by agreeing to hide the scale, you are colluding with her distress about weight. Although the scale is simply an objective monitor, there are times when she may perceive it as a benevolent friend who reassures her and, at other times, as a vindictive enemy who controls her. Her relationship to the scale is a volatile one. As with food, you don't want to get in the middle of it. Only she can find a way to peacefully coexist with the scale—or decide to get rid of it once and for all.

No Ifs, Ands, or "Butts"

"Honey, does this make my butt look big?"

OK—time to do things a little differently here. You're in the hot seat now and your challenge is to:

Come up with two inappropriate answers, which I suspect you will do brilliantly:

Come up with a helpful and empathetic response, for which I wish I could be a fly on the wall!

The Real Skinny

Let your honey be the judge of how well you do. But because she's still learning too, you may need to reference another scenario for confirmation.

So how'd you do? If you both feel you did well, bravo! That should earn you at least a kiss from your honey. If you didn't do so well, you will need to start reading from the beginning again—just kidding! As they say, it's simple but not necessarily easy. So hang in there and don't give up.

THE DANGER OF AN UNSUPERVISED EXERCISE PROGRAM...

FITNESS

TAE BO

CHAPTER FIVE

Getting Physical
When Exercise Is More than a Brisk Chat

Many individuals who are challenged by food and weight also struggle with exercise issues. These can range from being completely sedentary, to on-again, off-again exercise sprees, to the extreme of compulsive overexercising. All these behaviors are unhealthy to varying degrees.

Most of us are aware that exercise is good for us. Aside from weight management, the recognized benefits of exercise include increased energy, improved sleep, strong bones, and decreases in blood pressure, cholesterol, stress, anxiety, and depression. Not to mention the sheer pleasure of moving, breathing, and feeling connected to our bodies! But for the woman who is trapped in a pattern of abusive eating or poor body image, the goal of exercise is almost exclusively to become or stay thin. Improved health is often considered a side effect, not the primary goal.

Often, the more sedentary woman may make a valiant attempt to lose or manage her weight by initiating an intense exercise program. Too sudden and strenuous for her unfit body to tolerate, this may result in sore muscles, exhaustion, or even injury. As a result, she may give up and return to her sedentary lifestyle feeling like a failure. Over time, she may repeat this cycle again and again.

The woman more comfortable with exercise (but not with her weight) may use it as a means of purging her body of calories, warding off the terror of weight gain, or misguidedly attempting to feel more control over her life. Thinking "if some is good, more is better," she may feel compelled to endure longer and more intense periods of exercise. Then, instead of feeling more in control, her exercise regime may become compulsive and in control of *her*.

In contrast to these disturbed patterns of exercising and others like them, a healthy exercise program includes the following three ingredients:

- Variety, including aerobic, strengthening, and stretching routines
- Regularity, with a frequency of at least three times per week
- Healthy limits: no more than 2 hours per day

Keep in mind that these are general guidelines and vary based on individual needs, abilities and goals.

As you learn to stay out of your honey's decisions about food, it is also wise to stay out of her decisions about exercise—unless, of course, you think she has crossed the line and become a hazard to herself. Chapter Six will assist you in determining if she is in serious trouble and in need of professional help.

Honey...

Home Gym

Her treadmill, exercise bicycle, stair-stepper, Health Rider, NordicTrak, AbRoller, ThighMaster, etc. have taken over the garage, and she says: "Let's get an elliptical exerciser. I know I'd use it!"

Mocking: *"When pigs fly!"*

Don't be so negative! This could be the machine that actually works for her.

Off the mark: *"Why don't you just use the stuff you already have?"*

She has her reasons—do you really want to hear them all, including the critiques, rationalizations, and excuses related to each piece of equipment? Haven't you heard this already?

Closer to the mark: *"Sure, but first you need to sell all that equipment you aren't using."*

How likely is that?

Right on: *"If you really think you'll use it, it sounds like a good idea—as long as we can find a place for it."*

Mental Gymnastics

You may not believe this machine will be any different from the rest—and you could be right. But remember, if she exercises, you both benefit: she'll feel better about herself, be less stressed and irritable, have more energy, and live longer. Committing to an exercise program is not an easy task (consider all the gym memberships that go unused), and often involves many false starts. Most important is that she keeps trying, because one day it might stick. She'll need to find what works best for her, so don't discourage her from trying something new—assuming that your budget allows it, of course.

Personal $ Drainer

"I'm thinking of hiring a personal trainer—what do you think?"

First impulse: *"No way!"*

She's not asking for permission. She's asking your opinion. This reaction turns a conversation into a confrontation.

Think again: *"They're way too expensive."*

This could be money very well spent. Don't dismiss the idea too quickly.

Setting yourself up: *"You don't need to hire a trainer. I can help you workout."*

Really? You must know better by now!

Try this instead: *"That sounds like a good idea—if we can afford it."*

Mental Gymnastics

Personal trainers are definitely not cheap, but neither is blood pressure medication or bypass surgery. If she's not inclined to exercise on her own, a trainer may be just what she needs to get moving and get fit. If money is tight, how about looking at other ways you might be able to cut back and adjust the budget? This is a matter of her health, which should always be a priority. If she's someone who already exercises, a trainer can teach her proper form to prevent injuries, as well as help her develop new, well-rounded exercise routines that will keep it interesting. If she overexercises, feedback from a professional trainer can be an important and effective intervention. Recommend that she find someone with whom she feels comfortable and whose credentials, experience, and philosophy match her needs. Next to laughter, exercise (properly done) is the best medicine!

Too Fat to Exercise

"I'm too embarrassed to be seen exercising. I need to lose weight first!"

Challenging: *"That's just an excuse!"*

This may very well be true, but this type of direct confrontation is likely to trigger defensiveness rather than motivation.

Way out of line: *"You're not fat. You're just lazy."*

Do you really think this will inspire her to exercise? If so, think again!

Good try: *"No one is going to judge you. They'll be impressed that you're trying."*

Idealist! Wouldn't it be great if that were true? Unfortunately, we live in a fat-phobic culture, and she risks not only judgment but also ridicule.

Try this instead: *"Your health is much more important than what anyone thinks of you. But if you're that uncomfortable, you could consider joining a women's health club or doing exercise videos at home. Or maybe giving another go at some of the equipment that's in the garage."*

Mental Gymnastics

It's a shame she feels so bad about her body that she deprives herself of the benefits and joy of exercise. But if that is her truth, it's important to meet her where she is and not deny her feelings or try to make them go away. Her growth involves learning to care more about herself and less about what others think, and you can't do that for her. You can, however, model your own commitment to exercise and support whatever plan she decides to do. You can even offer to do some physical activities together! (See "Exercise Buddies" which follows.)

Exercise Buddies

"Honey, will you exercise with me?"

Not so fast: *"Sure!"*

Careful! If you're in better shape than she is, she may feel guilty because she's holding you back. Or she may get angry that she's about to collapse when you haven't even broken a sweat.

Think twice: *"No."*

She'll think you're not supporting her or that you don't want her to get in shape.

Try this instead: *"As long as you don't compare our fitness levels, I'd be happy to exercise with you, if it's something I enjoy doing or can get a workout from, too."*

Mental Gymnastics

If she's usually sedentary or feels intimidated or overwhelmed by the idea of exercise, the best thing you can do to support her is suggest activities to do together that don't necessarily feel like "exercising." They should be fun for both of you and require some physical exertion. Good examples are dancing, hiking, biking (consider a tandem bike), swimming, tennis, kayaking, skating or roller blading, or simply walking. You could also join a gym together and each work out at your own pace and level. If she finishes sooner than you, she can do some stretching or relax in the hot tub or sauna. Remember, you don't need to assume responsibility for her exercise or become her coach. Just support her by doing activities that you both enjoy.

Verbal Workout

She's a couch potato who jokes, "My idea of exercise is a brisk chat!"

Demeaning: *"That's ludicrous."*

Don't put her down: she's just being funny—and honest.

Sarcastic: *"And given how much you do it, it's a mystery you haven't lost any weight."*

Sarcasm can either be funny or offensive. She may think you're telling her that she talks too much and needs to lose weight.

Getting closer: *"And if it were an Olympic event, you'd take the gold!"*

Try this instead: *Smile and acknowledge her humor. Her joke is funny! Then you could tell her about exercise resistance syndrome.*

Mental Gymnastics

Exercise resistance syndrome is a concept that Francie White, M.S., R.D. (see *Resources*) defined as a conscious or unconscious block against becoming physically active. Rather than being "just lazy," women who are exercise resistant have usually had past experiences that interfere with their ability, willingness, or desire to exercise. Some examples of this are: being forced as a child to exercise in order to lose weight; having been shamed in gym class or while playing sports; receiving abusive treatment from a coach; suffering a serious exercise-related injury; or even having had an exercise addiction. Whatever the reason, every woman deserves to reclaim movement and activity as a natural and pleasurable part of being alive, without feeling compelled to do so or judged about it. Acquiring a psychological understanding of her personal history with exercise and separating exercise from weight management are two key steps to beginning to overcome exercise resistance. If your honey is serious about wanting to change, getting professional help will give her the best chance at a lifetime of healthful and joyful movement.

The Zen of Exercise

"Research has shown that you can build muscle just by visualizing it. I'm never going to the gym again!"

Unenlightened: *"That's cockamamie!"*
   Even if it is cockamamie, that's much too confrontational.

Judgmental: *"You are so gullible!"*
   That's a condescending put-down.

Good try: *"Don't forget to visualize cardiac fitness too!"*

That's the spirit: *"I'd like to see that research. It seems impossible!"*

Mental Gymnastics

It really does sound cockamamie and make her seem gullible, but this idea is actually true. A study conducted at the Cleveland Clinic Foundation in Ohio found that research subjects who participated in "imaginary" training sessions increased the muscle strength in their biceps by 13.5 percent—a rather amazing discovery and a reminder not to be so quick to judge! However, it's doubtful that visualization alone is enough for comprehensive fitness and the sense of well-being that comes from actual movement. So let's just trust that she's kidding about never going to the gym and hope she'll use visualization to enhance rather than replace exercising!

CHAPTER SIX

This Time I'm Serious

When Things Get Really Heavy

Despite the use of humor throughout this book, it is important to understand that food, weight and body image issues can become severe enough to interfere with everyday living. Those who have not experienced the struggle firsthand might have difficulty grasping the depth of pain, hopelessness, and shame that many women, and increasing numbers of men, are feeling. The mental, emotional, and physical suffering can be intense and debilitating. And, for growing numbers of individuals, the struggle does progress into a clinically diagnosable eating disorder such as anorexia or bulimia.

Because of shame or a need for control, your honey may be quite adept at hiding the severity of her symptoms. Denial and fear may cause her to minimize the behaviors or their effects, even to herself. She may even think that what she is doing is "acceptable" or "normal" because she may know other people who are doing the same things and our culture seems to glorify thinness at any cost. The longer the symptoms persist without intervention, however, the greater the toll they will take on her body, and the more difficult her recovery will be.

The physical complications of eating disorders are numerous, often chronic, and sometimes irreversible. They include gastrointestinal problems, esophageal rupture, cardiac problems, kidney damage, osteoporosis, loss of tooth enamel, amenorrhea (cessation of menstrual periods), and even death (anorexia has the highest mortality rate of all mental disorders). Eating disorders are usually accompanied by serious psychological problems, as well, such as depression, anxiety disorders, substance abuse, obsessive-compulsive disorder, and a history of sexual abuse, any one of which can be devastating by itself.

As the most intimate person in your honey's life, you are the one most likely to detect the signs and symptoms of an eating disorder—if you know what to look for and are willing to see. If you recognize any of the following scenarios, take immediate action because your honey is in significant trouble.

Honey...

Under the Knife

"I've finally found the perfect solution: gastric bypass surgery!"

Knee jerk reaction: *"Are you crazy?"*
  She's not crazy—but she may be desperate.

Overreacting: *"Over my dead body!"*
  That shows lots of passion, but let's hope there won't be *any* dead bodies involved!

Sincere but controlling: *"That scares me. I'd really rather you didn't do it."*

Try this instead: *"That's a life-threatening procedure. Let's research it together."*

But Seriously Now, Folks

Gastric bypass surgery is a medical procedure with a mortality rate between one and two percent. It is expensive and has a myriad of potentially dangerous, painful, and embarrassing side-effects. It also places tremendous stress on relationships and results in a high divorce rate. Some patients even develop health issues that require lifelong monitoring. It is not a panacea—even after the surgery, patients can (and often do) regain weight if they aren't mindful of food intake and exercise.

All that said, for some people gastric bypass is a lifesaver. If your honey is suffering health problems as a direct result of her weight, and all other avenues of weight loss have been exhausted, the procedure can help prolong, as well as improve the quality of her life. The decision to have surgery should not be made lightly.

Runaway Train

She's sick or injured but won't stop her strenuous exercise routine.

Bossy: *"You're never going to get better if you don't take care of yourself."*

She probably believes that exercising *is* taking care of herself.

Accusative: *"Why do you do this to yourself?"*

Compulsions are difficult to explain and to understand.

Audacious: *Forbid her from exercising.*

Nobody likes to feel controlled. She might exercise longer and harder just to defy you!

Try this instead: *Let her know you are concerned about how she is treating her body and ask her how she would respond if you or someone else she loved were doing the same.*

But Seriously Now, Folks

If she is a compulsive exerciser, trying to stop may be very difficult and can cause her intense anxiety, regardless of her condition. She may feel out of control or unconsciously fearful of difficult emotions that might surface, or she may be irrationally terrified of gaining weight. If her health or injury doesn't improve, she may hit bottom on her own. If her compulsive exercising persists and is accompanied by other dangerous behaviors (such as bingeing, vomiting, undereating, or severe weight loss), she may have a serious eating disorder. Let her know your fears and concerns and start researching treatment options.

Nothing to Lose

She has lost a significant amount of weight and become extremely thin, but she won't stop dieting.

Fat chance: *Tell her she's too skinny.*

A distorted body image will prevent her from believing you. She probably sees herself as fat even though she's thin.

Doomed to fail: *Tempt her with her favorite fattening foods.*

She'll interpret this as an attempt to sabotage her "success."

Try this instead: *Lovingly tell her you know how hard she's worked to lose weight, but now you are concerned that she is becoming anorexic. Let her know you are frightened, and request that you accompany her to a physician or therapist for an evaluation.*

But Seriously Now, Folks

Losing weight makes her feel good, powerful, and in control. It garners lots of praise and attention and bolsters self-esteem. Who wouldn't like that? But if her self-esteem was fragile to begin with, or she feels she's not in charge of her life, losing weight can become seductive and addictive. Like a powerful drug, it can affect her ability to reason and can even induce a state of euphoria. Therefore, it is critical that you intervene as soon as possible.

Urge to Purge

She keeps a large supply of laxatives (or emetics*) and goes through them quickly.

Unproductive: *Ask her why she needs them.*

This question gives her too much wiggle room. She can simply claim that she's constipated.

Invasive: *Throw them away.*

She'll just buy more and maybe hide them next time.

Try this instead: *"I've noticed that you use a lot of laxatives (or emetics). I'm concerned that this is a dangerous thing to do and that you may be using them for inappropriate reasons."*

*Emetics are substances that induce vomiting.

But Seriously Now, Folks

Frequent laxative or emetic use is a sign that she is attempting to manage her weight by purging unwanted calories from her system. However, these drugs don't really work for that purpose, and they can cause severe dehydration, physical dependence, and permanent damage. Laxative or emetic abuse is a symptom of bulimia and requires professional help. Again, you may find this behavior difficult to understand—even disgusting—but it's important to put your judgments aside so that you'll be able to help her. There's no doubt that she's embarrassed about this behavior—and about being caught. So she will need your support and compassion. Offer to see a therapist with her, and be firm about her need for help.

Consuming Passion

She frequently eats large amounts of food—even when she's not hungry—and feels painfully full, disgusted, or ashamed afterward.

Brain glitch: *"You eat like a pig!*

I don't need to tell you how far this comment will get you!

Ridiculing: *"Is there an upcoming famine I don't know about?"*

Don't be a smart ass!

On to something: *"Why don't you try eating only when you're hungry and stopping when you're full?"*

Great idea! But you can be sure that if it were that easy to change her behavior, she would have done it before now.

Try this instead: *"It makes me sad to see you suffer like this, and I'd like to help. Can we talk about possible solutions?"*

But Seriously Now, Folks

Her behavior is symptomatic of an illness known as binge eating disorder (see *Resources*). Although it may seem fairly benign, it's actually a progressive, debilitating illness. It is often accompanied by depression and anxiety, and can have serious medical consequences. She may think that the solution is to go on a diet, but that would address only the symptom rather than the underlying problem. Encourage her to seek professional help.

Losing It

She disappears into the bathroom shortly after every meal.

Reasonable but ineffective: *Ask her why she does this.*

If she is bulimic, her shame will prevent her from disclosing the truth. She will simply claim that she just "has to go."

Imposing: *Follow her into the bathroom.*

This is invasive and manipulative, and can only cause conflict and avoidance tactics.

Futile: *Try a distraction to prevent her from going.*

If you stand in her way, she may become uncontrollably anxious and fearful. She may even pick a fight in order to have a legitimate excuse to get away from you.

Try this instead: *After she returns, tell her you have noticed that she always goes to the bathroom after meals. Express that you are afraid she may have an eating disorder, offer your total support, and ask her if she is vomiting her food.*

But Seriously Now, Folks

Regular vomiting is a symptom of bulimia, a dangerous illness that can cause lasting health problems (see *Resources*). The longer she has it, the more difficult the recovery. As with laxative abuse, this behavior may be difficult for you to understand, but, if you want to help her, you must be compassionate. The symptoms of an eating disorder are expressions of underlying issues that she may not even be aware of yet. If she admits to being bulimic, offer to accompany her to a therapist. If she denies it, do some research on bulimia to find out about other symptoms that may clue you in. Confront her gently, but be persistent and adamant.

And One Pill Makes You Small...

You find a bottle of prescription or unmarked pills or some street drugs that she hasn't told you about.

Intrusive: *Confiscate it.*

Don't treat her like a juvenile delinquent. Remember, she's your partner, not your kid.

Reactive: *"What the hell is this?"*

Anyone who is approached with aggression is likely to become defensive or respond in kind.

Good try: *"Honey, have you been hiding something from me?"*

This is too vague and may confuse her—there could be a number of things she hasn't told you about!

Try this instead: *"I found your pills/drugs and am wondering why you've been using them—and hiding them from me."*

But Seriously Now, Folks

Abuse of diet pills, cocaine, methamphetamines, or any other stimulants or appetite suppressants is often brought on by poor body image and a desire to lose weight. Hiding drugs and using them in secret is a symptom of addiction. Lovingly express your concerns and invite her to talk to you about her drug use. It may be hard to know if she's using, abusing, or addicted, so you may need to consult a professional. If she admits that she's using the drugs to manage her weight, it's important to find a therapist who treats eating disorders and addictions. While there may be some crossover, the issues underlying *both* problems will need to be addressed.

Alien Visitation

You wake in the night to strange sounds and an eerie glow coming from the kitchen. You tiptoe down the hall to discover it's only her, eating in front of the open refrigerator.

Obvious: *"What are you doing?"*

That's not a helpful question unless you truly think she might be cleaning the refrigerator at 3:00 a.m. She's already embarrassed that you've seen her, and this question will further shame and humiliate her.

Not rocket science: *"You'll never lose weight like that."*

No one knows this better than she does.

Good try: *"Would you like me to pull up a chair for you?"*

This may seem polite, gentlemanly, and funny to you—but she'll probably think it's sarcastic and belittling.

Try this instead: *"Having trouble sleeping? Can I do anything for you?"*

But Seriously Now, Folks

Night eating can serve many different functions. Food can be a sleep aid for insomnia or a numbing agent for unresolved emotional issues that surface during sleep when defenses are down. Night eating can be a stress response or a primitive attempt at self-soothing (like a midnight breastfeeding). At best, it might simply be that she hasn't eaten enough food during the day! At worst, it might be a symptom of night eating syndrome (see *Resources*), a condition that may be related to a sleep disturbance. Since you don't know why she's eating, and she might not either, don't make assumptions. If it occurs frequently, suggest a professional evaluation.

Sugar Daddy

She's diabetic but doesn't adhere to her dietary guidelines, isn't monitoring her blood sugar, or goes into diabetic comas.

Shaming: *"Why can't you follow simple procedures?"*

The procedures may be simple, but they aren't necessarily easy. Don't be mean to her.

Antagonistic: *"Are you **trying** to kill yourself?"*

If this were a genuine suicide attempt, she'd probably use a more efficient means. You may be on the right track, however, because there may be unconscious reasons for her self-neglect.

Try this instead: *"I'm extremely worried and frightened by the way you're managing your diabetes. I don't want to lose you. How can I support you in taking care of yourself?"*

But Seriously Now, Folks

Even for people who aren't disordered eaters, sticking to a diabetic diet can be difficult. If your honey has an unusual relationship to food, this will be even harder. Facing her diabetes means she also has to face her food issues and their underlying causes, which can be scary and challenging. She will need help on two levels: 1) with the pragmatic aspects of managing her disease, and 2) with the emotional issues related to diabetes and to food. Her doctor and a dietitian should help with the former, and for the latter she can get help from a therapist, a diabetic support group, or an eating disorders support group. You can help her locate these as well as offering your own emotional support in her struggle.

Silent But Deadly

She has high blood pressure, and the doctor tells her she has to exercise regularly and lose weight.

Gloating: *"I told you so!"*

Has that statement ever achieved anything useful?

Alienating: *"Good! Maybe this will finally force you to lose some weight."*

She's upset enough about her new diagnosis. She doesn't need anything more to feel bad about.

Good try: *"We'll clean up our diet and exercise together."*

That's a sweet offer, but the motivation and commitment will have to come from her.

Try this instead: *"I'd like to support you in making these changes. Let me know how I can best do so."*

But Seriously Now, Folks

Hypertension is a significant condition that can cause dangerous health problems such as heart disease and kidney disease. Too often, people rely on medication alone as a treatment, disregarding the effectiveness of exercise and diet. Although hypertension usually has no noticeable symptoms, people usually feel significantly better when they make the behavioral changes that support good health. As a result, they often don't require medication. By now, though, you know that you can't make this decision for her. It's difficult to feel powerless when someone you love is sick, but remember that pushing, persuading, and shaming are not only ineffective, they may make her even more resistant to implementing necessary changes. Just let her know that you're there for her.

Inside Out

You see unusual or unexplained bruises or cuts on her body.

Ill-considered: *"Who have you been fighting with now?"*

A healthy sense of humor is great under the right circumstances, but these signs could indicate a serious problem that needs serious attention.

Self-centered: *"I don't know how you got those cuts and bruises—just don't go telling people I did that to you!"*

If you're always this insensitive, it's easy to see why she might want to blame you!

Good try: *"Has someone been hurting you?"*

Try this instead: *"I see you have cuts and bruises on your body. They look deliberate, and I'm very worried about you."*

But Seriously Now, Folks

Self-harm and self-mutilation are obvious indicators of emotional problems and should be addressed as soon as possible. Intentionally hurting herself can indicate a number of deep-seated issues: self-hatred, an attempt to feel something because she is emotionally numb, or an attempt to release or deflect emotional pain by incurring physical pain. She may not have any idea why she is doing it or why she can't stop, so don't get angry or press her to explain. If she admits that she is doing it, offer to help her find a therapist who has successfully treated people with these symptoms, and be sure not to treat her like she's crazy. She probably already feels crazy, and she needs to know that help is available and that you still love and respect her.

CHAPTER SEVEN

It's a Man's World
Or at Least It Used To Be

We all know the saying, "It's a man's world," referring to the power, privileges, and status men have generally enjoyed through the ages. This belief, however, discounts the lesser-acknowledged challenges, struggles, and suffering that accompany *being* a man in "a man's world." In most cultures, men are taught at a very early age to suppress emotions such as fear, grief, loneliness, and uncertainty. They are expected to present themselves to the world as strong, confident, and brave. Men have traditionally held the responsibility of being the sole providers for their families, have been the ones to go to battle during times of war, and have felt relentless pressure to be powerful and successful. At the same time, men have mercifully been spared most of the pressures of beauty and fashion, long viewed as the exclusive domain of women.

Times have changed, however. Today's men are also burdened by societal pressure to meet idealized standards of attractiveness—to dress fashionably and retain their youthful shape, vigor, smooth skin, and full heads of hair. Advertisers feature shirtless hunks and wistful, waif-thin youths. Cosmetics and grooming supply companies have developed successful lines of makeup exclusively for the male sex. The numbers of men electing to undergo plastic surgery procedures are skyrocketing. Chronic dieting, compulsive exercise, steroid use, and eating disorders accompanied by low self-esteem, lack of confidence, and shame have become increasingly serious problems.

Since women no longer hold a monopoly in this arena, they are in a unique position to help and support their men with food and body image challenges. This chapter will help women become aware of where some of these challenges lie. It will also provide tools and communication skills intended to prevent him from suffering the same fate as so many women.

No matter how tough your honey may appear to be, he too has his vulnerabilities and soft spots. So remember to be kind, gentle, and caring—without being coddling or condescending. As the person closest to him, you may have the privilege of being trusted with his most personal and intimate concerns. As a result, you can be very influential in helping him address these concerns while maintaining his dignity and sense of masculinity.

Honey...

Pumped

After three sessions with a personal trainer, he flexes his arm and says, "Honey, do my biceps look bigger?"

Inconsiderate: *"Not really."*

That might discourage him.

Well intended but misguided: *"Absolutely!"*

Are you telling the truth or just saying what he wants to hear?

Try this instead: *"I can't tell for sure, but it's certainly possible."*

The Long and Short of It

Society conditions men to believe they need to be "big and strong" in order to be manly. Fairy tales, movies, and novels portray the male protagonist as a hero who rescues the damsel in distress, beats up the bad guys, or saves the game with his athletic prowess. It's the skinny "loser" who gets the sand kicked in his face while the muscle man whisks away the girl. Some of the worst insults men endure involve being called a wimp, wuss, weakling, or sissy—names that challenge their masculinity and accuse them of lacking strength and courage. Consequently, the size of your honey's muscles may be intricately connected to his sense of manliness. So be sensitive in your response. Reassure him that you love his body just the way it is. Compliment him on other qualities that also reflect his masculinity, such as strength of character, nonviolent solutions to conflict, and perseverance when faced with challenges.

Small, Dark, and Handsome

He is self-conscious about his height and asks you not to wear high heels when you're out together.

Thoughtless: *"No one cares that I'm taller than you."*
  Obviously *he* does.

Belittling: *"You're being ridiculous."*
  You're judging and dismissing his feelings.

Good try: *"How about if we just don't stand close to one another while we're out?"*

Try this instead: *"If it's really important to you, of course I won't wear the heels."*

The Long and Short of It

We live in a culture that esteems and rewards tall men. They are more likely to be hired for jobs than shorter men and the taller presidential candidates usually win elections! Many women prefer a man they can "look up to." In fact, a woman once told me that because I'm only 5 feet tall, my 6'2" husband was a waste of a tall man! If your honey is sensitive about his height, be respectful and considerate of his feelings. Remember that he is the man you love, and his self-esteem is far more important than your desire to wear high heels (no matter how perfectly they go with your outfit). This one is really a no-brainer: just save the heels for an occasion when you're not together!

Size Doesn't Matter

He's curious about your ex and asks: "Was he bigger than me?"

Too hasty: *"Yes, he was pretty big."*

Careful—do you know what you are saying yes about?

Don't go there: *"What do you mean by bigger?"*

He'll take that to mean that at least *some* part of your ex was bigger.

Good try: *"Size doesn't matter."*

Not a very convincing statement. The jury still seems to be out on this one.

Try this instead: *"I don't compare you to him and wish you wouldn't either."*

The Long and Short of It

Clearly this is an ambiguous question. He could be asking about height, muscle mass, or even penis size. Regardless, your answer should maintain that comparisons never do anyone any good. (See "Does She or Doesn't She?" on page 24) Reassure him that you love him just the way he is. Remind him that he is the one you've chosen to be with, and the size of any particular body part has nothing to do with your reasons for loving him.

Try This On for Size

He's dressed for a special event and his clothes don't match, don't fit, or aren't appropriate for the occasion.

Critical response: *"You're not wearing that, are you?"*
He's got feelings too, you know.

Condescending: *"Didn't anyone teach you how to dress?"*
Obviously not, but there's no need to be mean.

Good try: *"Let's go see if we can't find something better for you to wear."*
A well-intentioned response, but definitely too maternal and judgmental.

Try this instead: *"Honey, you know that blue suit (or whatever) of yours? I think it would be just perfect for this event, and I love how good it looks on you."*

The Long and Short of It

During their formative years, men don't get nearly as much exposure to fashion as women, and they often don't know (or care) which colors go together, how to accessorize, or what length their pants and sleeves should be. Your honey may need some help in this department, but don't shame him about his appearance. Instead, make gentle suggestions about what looks good on him and offer to accompany him to shop for clothes. You can also buy him gifts of clothing that you know he will like and that will look good on him. Be sure to compliment him when he looks nice. Positive reinforcement goes a long way and is much more effective than criticism.

Scaling Mount Baldy

"Honey, I'm going bald! What do you think I should I do: try Rogaine, get a hair transplant, buy a toupee, or just wear my cap all the time?"

Callous: *"I'd try them all!"*

That sounds like you're as worried as he is, or you're laughing at his predicament.

Well-meaning: *"Go for the hair plugs—they'll last longer."*

It's his head and his decision to make. (Besides, they're painful.)

Missing the point: *"Why bother? It doesn't really matter."*

It matters to him!

Try this instead: *"I think you're attractive with or without hair, so do whatever you'll feel most comfortable with—or do nothing at all."*

The Long and Short of It

For centuries, a man's hair has been a symbol of power, virility, and youth. Remember the biblical story of Sampson? By cutting off his hair, Delilah deprived him of his strength and vitality. The emotional impacts of hair loss can include insecurity, panic, and a sense of loss. A receding hairline can provoke a man to face that he is growing older and will one day die. One study showed that balding men tend to have lower self-esteem, be less sociable, and suffer more from depression. So be sensitive to your honey's feelings and supportive of his attempts to deal with hair loss, even if they seem silly or unwarranted to you. Reassure him that you still find him handsome, sexy, and attractive no matter how much hair he has on his head.

Better Living through Chemistry

You find a bottle of Viagra in his nightstand drawer.

Tactless: *"What the hell is this?"*

Much too confrontational and definitely insensitive.

Oblivious: *"What do you need **this** for?"*

Do you really have to ask?

Try this instead: *"Honey, I'm sorry you felt you needed to hide this from me. Can we talk about it?"*

The Long and Short of It

Impotence is one of the most distressing personal problems a man can have. Erectile dysfunction (ED) causes frustration, humiliation, depression, anger, grief, loss, shame, guilt, and a heightened fear of rejection. Virility is deeply associated with masculinity, so its loss can make a man feel inferior. No wonder he didn't want to tell you about needing Viagra! ED can be caused by a variety of factors that include physical illness, injury, impeded blood circulation, psychological issues, and substance abuse. As many as one in ten men suffer from the disorder. If your honey hasn't yet discussed the problem with his doctor, encourage him to do so. Let him know that you will support him in every way possible because, in effect, his ED is also your ED. Most important of all, reassure him that you love him as much as you did before, and that you don't think he is any less of a man because of this difficulty.

Does This Make My Butt Look Big Enough?

"Honey, my butt is so flat that none of my pants fit right. Do you think I should get some of that underwear with a padded butt?"

Demeaning: *Burst out laughing.*
> He has dared to be vulnerable here, so be respectful.

Thoughtless: *"I thought they only made those for women."*
> That's emasculating.

Good try: *"Forget about it—you look fine."*
> Clearly he's unhappy so this may feel too dismissive.

Try this instead: *"I like your butt just the way it is, but if you think they'd make you look and feel better, it can't hurt to try."*

The Long and Short of It

Don't be too quick to dismiss his concern about his flat butt. Have you taken a good look at what he's talking about? Men's pants aren't designed for flat butts, so they tend to leave a lot of excess fabric just hanging around. In addition, men don't have indented waists. So without much of a butt, they have trouble keeping their pants up (often resulting in what's known as "plumber's butt"). Be sensitive about his concerns. They are no less valid than yours. You might also suggest that he consider suspenders. One suspender company even makes jeans especially for flat butts.

Supersize Me

He's eaten a hearty breakfast, a big lunch, and now he's eating a huge snack—right before you go out to dinner. He does this often and somehow never gains any weight.

Judgmental: *"I can't believe you're eating again!"*

Leave him alone—no one likes to have his eating monitored.

Cynical: *"One of these days all that food is going to catch up with you."*

Maybe so, but let him enjoy it while he can.

Meddlesome: *"You're going to spoil your appetite."*

"OK—Mom!"

Try this instead: *Don't say or do anything.*

The Long and Short of It

Admit it, you're jealous: jealous of his freedom with food, jealous that he can eat as much as he wants of whatever he wants and not think twice about it. It's just not fair! That's true, it's *not* fair. But there's a lot about life that's not fair, and this is really not one of the biggies. Rather than begrudging him his carefree eating, consider appreciating and celebrating his freedom with food. You may even be able to learn something from him that many women have forgotten: to eat when you're hungry and stop when you're full. The last thing you want to do is pick on his eating until he becomes as neurotic about food and weight as are so many women. Besides, his eating is not your responsibility, just like your eating is not his responsibility. Unless you seriously think he may have an eating disorder, keep your comments to yourself.

Hair, There, and Everywhere

You suddenly discover that he's got long hairs growing in his ears and nose, which he doesn't seem to have noticed.

Offensive: *Stare at his nose in disbelief.*
  That will only make him uncomfortable and self-conscious.

Overreactive: *"Oh my god! Look at your nose and your ears!"*
  Calm down, this is a treatable condition!

Good try: *"Honey, you might want to go look in a mirror."*
  Not specific enough.

Try this instead: *"Honey, it appears you've fallen prey to one of the more benign signs of aging: you have hair growing out of your ears and nose."*

The Long and Short of It

One of nature's cruel jokes on men is that, as they age, they lose the hair on their head and gain unwanted hair in their nose and ears. If your honey's eyesight is declining, there's a good chance that those hairs that seem so glaring to you may be difficult for him to see. Or perhaps he's never been one to spend much time examining his appearance in the mirror. You may need to gently remind him when it's time for a trim. To help him feel less awkward, be as nonchalant as you would when mentioning that it's time to mow the lawn. As a show of support, you could even buy him a really good "groomer."

Afterword

I hope you've enjoyed reading this book and that it has prompted a laugh or a smile even while treading on tender terrain. I also hope you are feeling somewhat enlightened about your honey's issues with food, weight and body image and the role that you play in that struggle.

As you now know, every time these issues arise you have a choice. You can respond in an ill-considered, insensitive or judgmental way that most likely adds to your honey's distress and distances you from one another. Or you can respond in a well-considered, supportive, esteem-building way that honors your honey's feelings, competence and independence and brings you closer to one another. The direction you choose can make all the difference. It's up to you.

Changing old patterns and behaviors takes time and practice. So be patient with your honey and yourself. If your situation feels too difficult to manage on your own, don't hesitate to ask for professional help. The sooner one gets support with any of the issues addressed in this book, including relationship skills, the greater the chances of improvement.

Lastly, whenever possible, remember to keep a sense of humor about life's challenges. The ability to laugh at ourselves makes life a lot easier and certainly a lot more fun. Peace.

Resources

Books

Anand, Margo. *The Art of Sexual Ecstasy*. Los Angeles, CA: Jeremy P. Tarcher, 1990.

Andersen, Arnold, Leigh Cohn and Thomas Holbrook. *Making Weight: Men's Conflicts with Food, Weight, Shape and Appearance*. Carlsbad, CA: Gürze Books, 2000.

Allison, Kelly C., Albert J. Stunkard and Sara L. Thier. *Overcoming Night Eating Syndrome: A Step by Step Guide*. Oakland, CA: New Harbinger Publications, 2004.

Burgard, Debra L. and Pat Lyons. *Great Shape: The First Fitness Guide For Large Women*. Lincoln, NE: iUniverse.com, 2000.

Comfort, Alex. *The Joy of Sex: Fully Revised & Completely Updated for the 21st Century*. New York, NY: Crown, 2002.

Fairburn, Christopher. *Overcoming Binge Eating*. New York, NY: Guilford Publications, 1995.

Freedman, Rita. *Bodylove*. Carlsbad, CA: Gürze Books, 2002.

Hall, Lindsey, and Monika Ostroff. *Anorexia Nervosa: A Guide to Recovery*. Carlsbad, CA: Gürze Books, 1998.

Hall, Lindsey, and Leigh Cohn. *Bulimia: A Guide to Recovery*. Carlsbad, CA: Gürze Books, 1999.

Hirschmann, Jane R., and Carol H. Munter. *When Women Stop Hating Their Bodies: Freeing Yourself From Food and Weight Obsession*. New York, NY: Fawcett Columbine, 1995.

Hochstrasser, April. *The Patient's Guide to Weight Loss Surgery:*

Everything You Need To Know About Gastric Bypass and Bariatric Surgery. Long Island City, NY: Hatherleigh Press, 2004.

Gaesser, Glenn A. *Big Fat Lies: The Truth About Your Weight and Your Health.* Carlsbad, CA: Gürze Books, 2002.

Levenkron, Steven. Cutting: *Understanding & Overcoming Self-Mutilation.* New York. NY: W. W. Norton & Company, 1998.

Lobue, Andrea and Marsea Marcus. *The Don't Diet, Live It! Workbook: Healing Food, Weight and Body Issues.* Carlsbad, CA: Gürze Books, 1999.

Maine, Margo and Joe Kelly. *The Body Myth: Adult Women and The Pressure to be Perfect.* Hoboken, NJ: John Wiley & Sons, 2005.

Phillips, Katharine A. *The Broken Mirror: Understanding and Treating Body Dysmorphic Disorder.* New York, NY: Oxford University Press, 1986.

Pope, Jr., Harrison G., Katharine A. Phillips and Roberto Olivardia. *The Adonis Complex: The Secret Crisis of Male Body Obsession.* New York, NY: Free Press, 2000.

Siegel, Michelle, Judith Brisman and Margot Weinshel. *Suriviving an Eating Disorder: Strategies for Family and Friends.* New York, NY: Harper Collins, 1997.

Tribole, Evelyn and Elyse Resch. *Intuitive Eating: A Recovery Book for the Chronic Dieter.* New York. NY: St. Martins Press, 1995.

Websites

www.ANAD.org
ANAD: National Association of Anorexia Nervosa & Associated Disorders provides information, referrals, education and support groups for eating disorders.

www.bettersex.com
The Sinclair Institute offers an excellent, unrated video series entitled, *The Better Sex Video Series*, produced in 2000.

www.bodypositive.org
A practical and informative website dedicated to "boosting body image at any size" through healthy living and size acceptance

www.gurze.com
This is the website for Gürze Books, a company that specializes in books, resources, and information about eating disorders.

www.nationaleatingdisorders.org
The National Eating Disorders Association offers educational materials and referral information, and promotes an annual Eating Disorders Awareness Week.

www.somethingfishy.org
A wonderful website full of information and resources for anyone concerned about eating disorders or suffering from them.

Acknowledgments

Essentially, this is a book about love. So, I'd like to thank those people in my life who have taught me the most about unconditional love.

First and foremost, with all the gratitude my heart has to offer, I thank my parents, my heroes, Eva and Joseph Hanich, who have never stopped loving me, no matter what, and who have never given up on loving each other for 66 years and counting.

My heartfelt thanks go to Tracy Parker (*mah freyen*), the quintessential friend, who I know beyond a shadow of a doubt, will always be there for me.

To Jerry Solomon, S.S.K., and B.H.D., who helped me learn how to love myself, and who live in my heart as a deep reservoir of comfort and validation, thank you.

And last, but most certainly not least, I am grateful to my husband, life's greatest gift to me, Robert G. Field, whose love nurtures and sustains me, and who effortlessly models unconditional love for all of humanity on a daily basis.

Special thanks go to my clients, whose challenges and courage have provided the very heart of this book; to my publisher and editor, Lindsey Hall, for her infectious enthusiasm, stalwart support, and brilliant guidance; to all the wonderful friends who helped me write, edit and persevere; and to my champion writers group, who helped make an author out of the world's most reluctant writer.

About the Author

Lydia Hanich is a licensed psychotherapist and frequent public speaker who specializes in eating disorders and body image issues. She obtained an M.A. in Counseling Psychology from the University of San Francisco, a B.A. in International Business and Language Area Studies from St. Norbert College, and is a Certified Eating Disorders Specialist through the International Association of Eating Disorder Professionals. She has lectured at conferences, taught workshops to both professionals and the public, and made appearances on local television and radio programs.

In addition, Hanich has lived and studied in Europe and Southeast Asia, and worked alongside Mother Teresa as a volunteer for the Missionaries of Charity in India. She has volunteered for the Red Cross Disaster Mental Health Team and the Santa Cruz AIDS Project Mental Health Providers. She has also served on the board of directors and as president of the Santa Cruz, California Association of Marriage and Family Therapists.

She currently lives in the Santa Cruz mountains with the husband of her dreams: a man who *didn't notice* that she had gained fifty pounds from the time they met to the time they married!

Order at www.gurze.com
or by phone (800) 756-7533

Honey, Does This Make My Butt Look Big? is available at bookstores and libraries and may be ordered directly from the Gürze Books website, *www.gurze.com,* or by phone (800) 756-7533.

FREE Catalogue
The *Eating Disorders Resource Catalogue* features books on eating and weight related topics, including body image, size acceptance, self-esteem, and more. It also includes listings of nonprofit associations and treatment facilities and is handed out by therapists, educators, and other health care professionals around the world.

www.gurze.com
Go to this website for additional resources, including many free articles, hundreds of books, and links to organizations, treatment facilities, and other websites.

Gürze Books has specialized in eating disorders publications and education since 1980.